Praise for
Clear Leadership

"In a time when everyone knows they need to 'get different' in their interactions and in the workplace, Bushe has given us a road map with plenty of examples."

Frederick A. Miller, CEO, The Kaleel Jamison Consulting Group, Inc.;
coauthor, *The Inclusion Breakthrough* and *Be BIG: Step Up, Step Out, Be Bold*

"A wise teacher, Bushe first takes us by the hand and patiently leads us deep into the mush that constitutes so much of the noncommunication of organizational life. Then, after we have recognized ourselves as the creators of that mush, he gives us the knowledge and practical tools we can use to break through the mush and create the clarity essential to effective leadership."

Barry Oshry, president, Power & Systems Inc.; author, *Seeing Systems: Unlocking the Mysteries of Organizational Life*

"*Clear Leadership* is a thoughtful and thought-pr━━━━━ ━k explaining how to untangle the hidden mush and brus━━━━━━━━━━ ━, your team's, and your organization's effectiveness. I━━━━━━━━━━ ━n of theory and practice with extensive examp'━━━━━━━━━━━━━━ excellent resource for anyone who wan━━━━━━━━━━━━━━━━ ━g with others at work and at home."

Robert J. Marshak, author, *C━━*

"*Clear Leadership* provides new co━━━━━━ ━o the thinking on leadership. The skill sets are not just for leaders, ━━ ━or everyone engaged in partnering with others to accomplish something; and in today's world, leading learning is just as important as leading performing."

David W. Jamieson, PhD, president, The Jamieson Consulting Group, Inc.; adjunct professor of management, Pepperdine University; adjunct professor, American University/NTL Institute MSOD Program

"Rarely does one find a business model with as much impact on human behavior in the work of transforming relationships and organizations as the 'experience cube.' This masterful and ingenious creation of Gervase Bushe has without reservation been our model of choice in dealing with executives and their aversion to having difficult and authentic conversations. I am in awe with the feedback our company receives after introducing the 'experience cube' to organizations and their leadership teams."

Greg W. Nichvalodoff, president, Inscape Consulting Group Inc.

"Bushe offers lessons for handling the most pressing problem for knowledge-based organizations—organizational mush. He goes beyond the question of what is taking place in troublesome partnerships and looks into the essential question of how to be a competent partner and collaborator. Brilliant and utterly useful. In Scandinavia, many of our most committed and skillful leaders within business, civil service, and politics apply the theory and practice of clear leadership."

Anders Risling, PhD, licensed psychologist; founder, Provins fem